SPEAK
—— like ——
MAGIC

6 SECRET STEPS for making powerful presentations to PLEASE your audience

AARON O'BRIEN

TESTIMONIALS

"
I wish I had this book 40 years ago! Aaron's concise and compelling tips will make my next presentation even better. I highly recommend this book to those just launching a speaking career—or people who need to do more audience-centric presentations. His insights about how to do effective Zoom meetings are especially poignant today.
—JAY MINCKS, Executive Vice President, Insperity
"

"
Wow! It's so great when you find a book that completely drags you in and directly speaks to you, it blew my mind and managed to surpass my highest expectations. Public Speaking is listed as America's #1 fear, people are actually less afraid of dying. Aaron magically uses his genius of simplicity and guides you to overcome your greatest fear, dialing you in to a heightened confidence you never knew you had.
**—GARRY COLLETT,
Founder, California Commercial Investment Companies**
"

> The best part about Aaron's speaking secrets is that every step is scalable, whether your audience is big or small, virtual or face-to-face. This book will help you level up your presentation skills from just talking AT people to drawing in your audience to EXPERIENCE your story.
> —**KIRHAN CHENG**, Corporate Meeting Planner

> "PLEASE" read this book and you'll be inspired by Aaron's methods that leave audiences spell-bound. Aaron understands people and lays out concrete steps that will allow you to better connect with your audience using empathy and empowerment. I love his approach because it requires genuine regard for others and is not about pure self-promotion. I've been privileged to see Aaron turn regular moments into once-in-a-lifetime experiences using the techniques discussed in this book. Aaron is working hard to fan his gifts into flames—and the world is better for it.
> —**DARREN KERSTIEN,**
> Corporate Attorney, Gibson, Dunn & Crutcher LLP

TABLE OF CONTENTS

FORWARD: WHO IS THIS KID? By Adam Christing — 11

INTRODUCTION: THE MAGIC WORD THAT HELPS YOU SPEAK LIKE MAGIC! — 15

CHAPTER 1: PERSONALIZE YOUR MESSAGE FOR THEM — 19

CHAPTER 2: LISTEN TO THEIR PAIN — 29

CHAPTER 3: EMPOWER THEM TO WIN — 39

CHAPTER 4: AUTHORIZE THEM TO MOVE FORWARD — 47

CHAPTER 5: SHOW THEM IT WORKS — 57

CHAPTER 6: ENCOURAGE THEM TO GO FOR IT — 65

BONUS CHAPTER: TEN TIPS FOR HOW TO SPEAK LIKE MAGIC IN VIRTUAL SETTINGS — 73

YOUR ONE-PAGE "CHEAT SHEET" SPEECH OUTLINE — 78

ACKNOWLEDGMENTS — 81

INSPIRE MAGIC AT YOUR NEXT EVENT! — 85

SPEAK LIKE MAGIC: Six Secrets for Making Powerful Presentations to PLEASE Your Audience

© 2021 Aaron O'Brien

All rights reserved. No part of this book may be reproduced or transmitted in any manner without the express written consent of the publisher, except in the case of brief excerpts in critical reviews or articles. All inquiries should be addressed to P.O. Box 175, 1534 N. Moorpark Road, Thousand Oaks, CA, 91360-5129.

This publication is designed to provide accurate and authoritative information in regard to the subject matter covered. It is sold with the understanding that neither the publisher nor the author is engaged in rendering legal, accounting, or other professional service. If legal advice, psychological advice, or other expert assistance is required, the services of a competent professional person should be sought. *Adapted from a Declaration of Principles Jointly Adopted by a Committee of the American Bar Association and a Committee of Publishers and Associations.*

Published in the United States by *Inkredible Books*.

This book may be purchased in bulk at special discounts for sales promotion, corporate gifts, fund-raising, or educational purposes. Special editions can also be created to specifications. For details, contact hello@aaronobrien.com.

To book Aaron O'Brien for speeches or performances, contact Brian McElreath at brian@aaronobrien.com or call: 707-774-5184.

Cover and interior design by Lisa Barbee, DesignsDoneNow.com
Edited by Kristi Hein, PicturesandWords.com
Author photo by David Muller, DavidMullerPhotography.com

Print ISBN: 978-1-7362126-0-8
Ebook ISBN: 978-1-7362126-2-2

Printed in the United States of America

10 9 8 7 6 5 4 3 2 1

DEDICATION
For Hailey

FOREWORD

Who is this kid, Aaron O'Brien?

The first time I met Aaron O'Brien was in Las Vegas. I was attending Magic Live, North America's largest annual magic convention, which attracts wonder-workers from around the globe.

There were several thousand magicians in attendance. But when my friend David Doyle introduced me to Aaron, I noticed something different about him. While other magicians were buying shiny props, making coins and cards disappear, and trying to impress each other with finger-flinging sleight-of-hand moves, Aaron had a different magical quality. Though only seventeen at the time, Aaron was already a *dynamic communicator*.

He spoke with confidence. His words were charged with enthusiasm. And unlike most high school students, who gaze mostly at their phones, Aaron looked people right in the eye and paid attention to what they had to say. I thought to myself: *Who is this kid?*

Turns out, Aaron and I had a lot in common. We both grew up at the world-famous Magic Castle in Hollywood, California. The Magic Castle is the legendary clubhouse of the Academy of Magical Arts and is considered the mecca for magicians. Within this special club is yet another club that is quite prestigious: the Junior Society for performers aged thirteen to twenty.

Many of the finest magicians working today have come through this exclusive group. Aaron was admitted at the age of thirteen. I passed the audition myself (barely) at the age of seventeen back in the 1980s. Now, four years after meeting this "kid" in Las Vegas, I can point to three qualities I most admire in Aaron O'Brien:

At twenty-one, Aaron is already a tremendous professional speaker. He is super-enthusiastic about helping other people become powerful presenters.
Aaron is the real deal.

He has spent hundreds of hours presenting on stages—and in Zoom Rooms—perfecting the very speaking secrets he shares with you here. I know he has poured his heart and soul into this book.

Study after study confirms it: most people are afraid to speak in public. This book will go a long way toward making that fear disappear. Aaron's six secrets will help you prepare and present a dynamic speech or other presentation. Plus, he offers tons of tips for knowing what to say to your audience and how to say it.

You are about to discover a step-by-step formula for designing and delivering a talk that is *amazing*. You will love it. I hope you use it every time you speak to an audience of any size.

I lead a speaker/entertainment bureau called *Clean Comedians*. We represent dozens of talented performers and speakers who believe humor doesn't have to be filthy to be funny. Aaron has quickly become a favorite presenter with our meeting and event coordinators, including several Fortune 500 companies. When an organization books Aaron to speak or entertain, two things happen: First, he amazes their group. Second, he gets invited back.

Magicians are not supposed to reveal their secrets. Fortunately for us, Aaron is spilling the beans about the real magic behind inspiring and impacting people with your words—whether that's from a stage or on a screen.
So, *who is this kid?* Let me rephrase that question.
Who is this young man? Here's the answer: Aaron O'Brien is a rising star in multiple worlds: speaking, entertainment, and publishing. This is his first book. I know it won't be his last.

If you want to become a powerful presenter, you've come to the right place. I am sure you will enjoy *Speak Like Magic*. And more important, I am confident that, if you read this book and implement Aaron's speaking secrets, you will become a better communicator. Every time you deliver a talk, make a sales presentation, give a speech, or do a wedding toast, you can amaze your audience too.

Happy reading!

—ADAM CHRISTING

Adam Christing is the founder of CleanComedians.com. He is the author of three humor and personal growth books and has been ranked among the top five after-dinner speakers in the U.S.

INTRODUCTION

Want to become an *amazing* speaker?

I learned how. You can, too.

I am a professional speaker, magical entertainer, and emcee. In the last nine years, I have been in front of nearly every kind of business, educational, and non-profit group you can imagine. And after giving more than a thousand presentations, I've written this book for you to share what I have discovered.

I have made every mistake a presenter can make. But along the way, I have been mentored by some of the finest entertainers, speakers, executives, and salespeople around. And I have learned some incredible secrets about the art of communicating with people.

Now, my goal is simple: *I want to help you become a fearless, focused, and fantastic speaker.*

Are you ready to learn to Speak Like Magic?

This short book can be your blueprint for giving energizing presentations, and I am honored to be your guide. I am excited to help you discover a very special step-by-step process for creating killer presentations.

Note: You *already* know how to speak. You do it every day. But this book will help you speak with a new sense of confidence and clarity. I'm going to show you exactly how to design and deliver strong messages.

This book is for salespeople, business leaders, teachers, preachers, marketers—anybody who wants to communicate person to person. I will reveal six secrets to pleasing your audience every time you give a speech, make a pitch, or deliver a presentation.

I have been performing magic tricks since I was twelve years old. People love magic. And it's an awesome feeling when you find you can amaze other people. But you don't have to be a professional magician to learn to Speak Like Magic. When you bring your unique expertise and enthusiasm to the techniques you'll learn here, soon you will be blowing your audience away with what *you* have to say and how *you* say it.

You can learn how to become a dynamic speaker in front of live or online audiences. I'll be showing you the tips and tricks I have discovered through making presentations to audiences ranging in size from two to two thousand. I will also help you avoid common mistakes that speakers make. But beyond learning the tricks of the trade, I want to share one powerful *magic word* with you. This word forms the outline for this book.

THE MAGIC WORD

Sometimes I will invite an audience to "Shout out some magic words!" You might guess some of the words they shout: *"Abracadabra!* "Hocus-pocus!" "Shazam!" "Open sesame!"* I even hear things like *"Money!"*

"Wine!" and *"Netflix!"* But there's *one* word more powerful than all of those "magic" words combined. It's a word you first learned as a child.

Remember *the* word Mom would remind you about? She'd ask: "Can you say *please*?" You learned to say please and started using this amazing word every single day. You said "please," and your mom smiled, your teachers were impressed, and you often found yourself getting exactly what you asked for. In these pages, PLEASE is both our powerful magic word and an acronym for learning to Speak Like Magic. Here's how you will PLEASE your audience:

Personalize your message for them.
Listen to their pain.
Empower them to win.
Authorize them to move forward.
Show them it works.
Encourage them to go for it.

This book has no fluff. It's packed with practical ideas that really work. Each step of our magic word PLEASE is a new chapter you'll dig into. PLEASE is also the six-step sequence you can use to prepare and present an awesome speech.

Next time you are preparing a talk, you won't have to guess how to outline it. You'll use the PLEASE sequence to craft an amazing presentation.

In my work as a professional speaker and entertainer, I have been in front of screaming kids at birthday parties, distracted executives at Fortune 500 companies, and everything in between. Guess what? The PLEASE formula works in any setting. This method will work for you whether your next talk is in a ballroom, classroom, or boardroom.

Maybe you've already noticed this: Each part of the PLEASE outline is designed outwardly—to serve your audience. It's not all about *me*, it's all about *them*. I believe this is the secret ingredient not only for giving great talks, but also for improving your communication skills.

I conclude each chapter with three tools for your talk, key ingredients for designing and delivering a great speech. I've also provided space for you to write down your own takeaway for each chapter.

At the end of the book, you'll find a bonus chapter to help you Speak Like Magic for your next Zoom, virtual, or online presentation.

And finally, I've provided a "Cheat Sheet" outline you can use to quickly create your next presentation using my six-step sequence. You will PLEASE your audience.

I love my job. And I'm so excited to share these six powerful presentation secrets with you.

Say the magic word, and let's turn the page together. It's time for you to become a more powerful presenter. Let's discover how to Speak Like Magic.

LET'S GO!

Here's to your speaking success.

—AARON O'BRIEN
Thousand Oaks, California

P.S. In that spirit, please know that I am here to be of service to you. If you have questions about any of this material, you are welcome to email me: Aaron@AaronObrien.com. I'd love to hear from you. And please share your speaking success stories with me. I know you will begin to amaze your audiences from our time together.

CHAPTER 1
PERSONALIZE YOUR MESSAGE FOR THEM

> *Personalization is pointless without knowing the individual. Understand the dreams, hopes, and fears that motivate your customers, then hit them where it counts.*
> **—PAUL GILLIN, The Daily Carnage**

I wasn't sure I could pull it off.

As a twenty-one-year-old, how was I going to connect with a group of employees who had been working in the corporate world for longer than I had been alive?

I had been hired by Fidelity to give an entertaining presentation. Yes, that Fidelity—the Fortune 500 multinational financial services company that manages assets of $3.2 trillion. (I had less than .00000000000000001% of that in my bank account.)

My job? To entertain and inspire their call center employees who support financial advisors. What if I bombed? What if they saw through me? What if they stopped me during my speech and said, "Why should we listen to him?" I designed my presentation, said a little prayer, and went for it.

Fidelity was having a difficult time raising morale in their team. They needed someone to come in and bring some much-needed laughter to their group. I started the event by asking their team to share some of the challenges they were going through and needed help navigating. This allowed me to customize my presentation for their event and help them meet their needs.

Thankfully, I slayed them. I was able to use the six secrets I will show you in this book to help make my presentation about the audience and not about me (more on that soon). The Fidelity manager was thrilled. He sent me a special word of thanks and said my presentation was exactly what his people needed.

Let me explain: "Slaying" is a good thing in this situation. My magician friends at the Magic Castle like to say, after they come off the stage, "I just slayed 'em." Professional comedians say, "I destroyed." Many speakers say, "Knocked 'em dead." You don't need to use a violent word. You can say "I rocked them." Whatever you say, the key is to make sure you wow them.

HERE'S HOW
Here's secret #1 in our PLEASE program. You need to personalize your communication. Make your message for and about them, not you. Let me repeat this because it's exactly what you want to do as you are preparing your next presentation. Make it all about them! When you personalize your message to your audience, they are going to know that you care and that you are paying attention to them.

That's what I did with Fidelity. I was able to connect with their great team and create a fun experience during a difficult time—because I made it all about them. I asked their organizing team questions about the area they live in, such as favorite sports teams and favorite restaurants. I also asked for any internal lingo they could reveal to me (they were not allowed to reveal much, as they handle some very private data).

During the initial call with the client and my booking agent Brian McElreath with *Clean Comedians,* I made it clear: I avoid these 3 P's: profanity, prejudice, and politics. When personalizing a presentation, it is key to know any topics the client would like you to avoid, so you do not offend anyone. Always err on the side of caution.

Here's the point of personalization. When you buy a picture frame, you don't hang up the frame with the stock photo of a generic happy family. You replace that with a photo of your family that you took at Grandma's barbecue last year. Similarly, in the real world of connecting with an audience, you need a personally crafted message that is all about them.

FLIP THE SPOTLIGHT AROUND

As an entertainer, I had to learn to do something that's very uncomfortable for most performers. I had to learn to flip the spotlight away from me and onto my audiences. Fact is, this is what makes for the best speeches. When you shine the light on them and deliver a message that applies to them, it changes something for them. (Notice how many times I said "them.") You have made them the stars!

The first step in making your message all about your audience is to go back to basics. Determine the why and what before you decide the how. To know your mission, you must get clarity about why you are speaking to this person, group, or audience.

Maybe you've heard the saying "Begin with the end in mind." That's just what you need to do: begin with the end of your speech in mind.

When you get to the end of your talk, what will you be asking your audience members to know, believe, and act on?

Preparing your presentation is like driving. Think about where you are going. You are about to invite your audience to jump into the car with you. So put your destination into your GPS.

Here are some questions you can ask yourself to help you get to know your audience and personalize your message for them:

- WHO is my audience?
- WHAT is the message they need at this time?
- HOW will I help them achieve their goals?
- What am I asking them to DO?

There's a classic bit of advice for public speakers that's probably been true for centuries: know your audience. There are many levels to this. For me, it's not only What does this company do? (though that's important). It's why do they do it? How do they do it? And here is where the rubber meets the road in your messaging: What are the names of the people in my audience?

Whenever possible, even if it's a group of more than a hundred people, I love to get a list of names long before I speak. Many meeting planners will also provide me with links to attendee photos.

Why is this so important? I'll tell you why in three words: Learn. Their. Names.

You might be asking How do you learn and remember people's names? Okay, this might sound crazy from a twenty-one-year-old, but I don't just use my phone. I found an old invention that also works great for me: a small pad of paper and a pen.

I carry a little notepad, and I write down the names of people in my audience before I speak with them. There is something that happens in the brain when you apply physical pen to paper to write down their names. I love to write down the names of people I meet, and then when I go to give a speech, I refer to them by their names.

When you remember the name of their organization and the names of attendees, it's magical. It's so powerful. When you learn a person's name and use it with them, you are making a huge statement to them. You are saying I am invested in you.

This is a power move both on and off the stage (or on screen)! People don't think to tap into this amazing power. But imagine never again being that person who has to ask someone their name again and again at a dinner party.

Many people say they're bad at remembering names, but the truth is they don't forget others' names—they never learn them to begin with. If, when you first meet someone or even before you give a speech, you're thinking to yourself *Well, I'm not going to remember their name*, then you're right: you won't. But imagine if you take that extra beat and reinforce to yourself *Oh, she said her name was Terry.*

Don't rush ahead in the conversation. Make it a point to mentally pause over people's names.

There are a handful of tricks to help you remember names in any circumstance.

First tip: Study names before you ever hit the stage (or your virtual platform).

The first step is knowing who will be in your audience.

Take the time before you go into conversation, before you go into a presentation, to study those things and spend the extra ten, fifteen, twenty minutes to focus on these wonderful people.

Second tip: Say aloud as many people's names as possible.

Right away, try to use the person's name in conversation—and in your speech.

The first time I was on television, I was nervous. You know what helped me? Mentioning the host's name: Tim. Now, I did make the mistake of repeating the host's name too many times because I was nervous. But it showed the audience at home that I was invested and was able to connect with him.

It's important to say their name a few times in conversation. For example: I'm at a networking event, and I meet Terry. She tells me she works for Chase Bank. I might say, "Great to meet you. How long have you worked at Chase, Terry?"

Third tip: Use a special memory technique.

After listening to Terry's answer, and possibly repeating it back to her in my own words, I come up with a mnemonic trick to help remember her name.

POWER POINT: MNEMONICS

How do you say mnemonics? I pronounce it: "new-monicks." But that's just me. What's important is not how you say it, but that you use it. Mnemonics is a shortcut for your brain to help you remember names, faces, key words, and more. This special technique will help you remember (and speak) like magic.
Want to learn more? Read *The Memory Book: The Classic Guide to Improving Your Memory at Work, at School, and at Play* by Harry Lorayne and Jerry Lucas.

Using the example of Terry, I paint a visual image connected with this person named Terry.

On first hearing "Terry" I visualize her name: TERRY.

To me, that sounds a lot like "tree," so I imagine Terry as a tree! She has curly hair, so I see those curls as leaves. I want to make sure I get a picture in my mind, because our brains think not in words, but in pictures.

As I get to know Terry, I discover that she loves In-N-Out hamburgers. So I see her face on a giant tree with double-double burgers growing out of her hair. Of course, I don't tell Terry what I'm seeing. I make the picture as ridiculous as possible (the more ridiculous, the better), which helps me remember her name.

It might sound crazy, but this mental exercise can help you remember almost anything. Feats of memory like memorizing cards, lists of words, digits in long numbers...even trivia facts, if associated with an outrageous visual image, become unforgettable. Just let your imagination create a comical larger-than life image.

Fourth tip: What is the message they need at this time?

SPEAK *WITH* THEM BEFORE YOU SPEAK *TO* THEM
Think about the kinds of questions you can ask that will help you gain understanding, and then weave the answers you get into your presentation. Ask:

- What is your goal for this program? How many attendees? Tell me about them. What challenges are your people facing?
- Who are some key team members I can incorporate into my talk? What are their names?
- Tell me about your culture, and please include some internal lingo.

Fifth tip: Speak their language.

This is another opportunity to get to know your audience. If you want people to feel connected to you, become familiar with their internal jargon and culture.

Before I address a group, I ask them to tell me a little bit about how their group communicates. I have the privilege of speaking frequently to the sales teams at Insperity. I know their language. They don't call their sales reps "salespeople." They are BPAs (Business Performance Advisors).

I am not an employee of Insperity. But I have absorbed their words, acronyms, and language into my presentations for them. Recently, one of Insperity's managers asked me, "How long have you worked for Insperity?" This is one of the biggest compliments I can receive as a speaker. You may be making your presentations internally to an organization, but the same concepts apply. You want your audience to feel like: *Wow. She really gets us. How is she able to read my mind?*

When you customize your talk so that it's about their organization, their people, their names, their unique language, and their needs, you not only will have their attention—you will keep it. And the impact of your presentation will be huge. It will be magical.

Dig up some inside jokes. Do you have inside jokes with certain friends? It creates a warm connection between you and your friend, right? It's the same thing with an audience.

I'll wrap up this chapter with one of the greatest quotes you will ever read. This wisdom applies to life and designing a superb speech. I encourage you to read it twice. (Bonus points if you read it aloud.)

> *I've learned that people will forget what you said,*
> *people will forget what you did,*
> *but people will never forget how you made them feel.*
> **—MAYA ANGELOU**

TOOLS FOR YOUR TALK

- Weave their names into your message.
- Learn and speak their language.
- Make their goal the mission of your message.

My personal takeaway:

_____

_____

_____

_____

_____

CHAPTER 2
LISTEN TO THEIR PAIN

> "
> *People don't care how much you know until they know how much you care.*
> **—THEODORE ROOSEVELT**
> "

He is the wealthiest man on the planet.

How did Jeff Bezos, the founder of Amazon, do it?

According to leadership expert and Inc. writer Justin Bariso, it boils down to three words that Bezos cited in a 2000 television interview. What are the three key words that catapulted Amazon to become the biggest business in the world? Bezos says they are *listen*, *invent*, and *personalize*.

Notice that Jeff Bezos puts listen before invent. Another secret that will help you Speak Like Magic. Bezos built Amazon based on the pain he was hearing from others—about how difficult it was to buy books without driving miles away from your home.

> **FUN FACT**
> You are reading *Speak Like Magic*. Get this: Before Bezos named his company Amazon, he wanted to use a magical name: Cadabra!

He listened to customers. He felt their pain. And he created a powerful solution that now works like magic. I love Amazon. Search for what you need. Click the purchase button. Two days later it arrives at your house. That's (near-)instant gratification.

But don't be fooled. Bezos' success did not come first from its amazing delivery system, though it is amazing. The success of Amazon is based on how incredibly customer-centric the company is for millions of users. Bezos created a way for those people to get what they needed right away. Again, it started with listening.

Now, not everybody is a fan of Jeff Bezos. There's no denying that on its path to global success, Amazon has toppled many small businesses. The point for this book, though, is that the most powerful business in the world started by deeper listening.

So let's take Bezos' breakthrough and apply it to you. How can this help you prepare and deliver a powerful talk? Bezos said, "First you have to listen to customers." And he added another key: "Second, you have to invent for customers, because companies that only listen to customers fail. It's our job at Amazon to invent…those kinds of things that customers really like."

Like Jeff Bezos, you must reverse-engineer your presentations. He put it this way: "Leaders start with the customer and work backward."

Finally, there's personalization. We've already unpacked its power in the previous chapter. Let's take another look, with Bezos' success in mind.

You and I may not become billionaires, but we can become more customer-centric. Here's how: Before you invent your talk, find out what your audience needs. You must discover what struggles they are experiencing. As you develop your speech, concentrate on how you can present a message to your audience that will actually help them.

First, discover where they are hurting. What kind of jam are they in?

Examples:

- Are they hurting physically or emotionally in some tangible way?
- Is their group facing a specific money or time challenge?
- Will there be consequences for them if they do not fulfill a personal or business goal (for example, a sales or productivity target)?

BECOME A PAIN DETECTIVE
Identify their needs before you prepare your talk. Don't make the mistake of writing out your talk before doing a deep dive into your listeners' problem(s)—you might end up having to write another speech!

Save yourself some time; personalize before you start writing. Do your homework. Engage in some pre-presentation Zoom sessions or phone calls with those in the know. Become a pain "detective." After you make some discoveries, prepare your presentation around the key hurting point(s).

Most speakers come across as boring not because they can't speak well, but because they don't understand where their audience is struggling. To paraphrase Teddy Roosevelt, people won't care about your presentation unless you show them you care about their problem.

Important note: Stay current. And keep things appropriate. The point of your talk is not to bring up old hurts, resentments, or bitter memories. You don't want to reopen old wounds. Be direct. Ask the person who invited you to speak, "What are you all struggling with right now?" The point is simple: You want to help them.

Here's exactly what you can say before you design and deliver your speech. "I'm so excited to be able to help your group. Can you tell me about the biggest challenge your team is facing at this time? Please be specific."

Here's a funny text exchange about how much people want to be listened to:

iMessage
Today 12:20 PM

I am here for you

Thanks :) I'm going through a tough time so it means a lot

And sorry, I lost all my contacts. Who is this?

This is your Uber driver

I am here to pick you up

Oh

Delivered

It's funny, but it's more than just funny. The point of this conversation, for purposes of your presentation, is that everyone in your audience needs to hear that you are there for them. Tell them you are happy to listen to what they have going on in their life. This shows you just what kind of value you bring to your audience by simply listening to them.

In life we tend to hear the words that are being said but do not understand the real message. It will enhance your speech to clarify the situation before jumping in with both feet or, in this case, with your mouth.

Listening to their pain means entering into their world. This requires mutual vulnerability.

You must (gently) uncover the suffering or potential suffering. And remember, sometimes people want to gossip or just vent. That's not what you are after here. You are *not* entering into a therapy session as a speaker. You are delivering a message. This part of your presentation is about stating what needs fixing. Speaking like magic means helping other people understand how to make their problems disappear.

Magic happens for your audience when you make it clear that you know what's wrong. And they see that you have a plan for making things better. We are wired as emotional beings, so be careful about working up a logical solution to a relational or motivational problem. If you are preparing a message about the importance of paying your taxes on time, you don't want to say, "It's the law." That is logical. You want to say, "If you don't pay your taxes on time, you will experience fears, fines, and the wrath of the IRS." Now they will be ready to hear your solution.

Here are the three steps to listening to their pain that you should follow as you are preparing your talk.

#1. Identify Their Struggle
Struggle is a strong word. I'm using it on purpose. If you don't know where your audience is hurting then you won't be able to guide them to experience relief.

Many people hide their struggles in life behind a facade of having it all together. As a speaker, you are there to help them experience authentic change. To do that, you must first know what struggles your audience members are dealing with. This will enable you to give them the right help.

To illustrate this, here is a funny story from Murray Grossan, MD, founder of the Grossan Institute, Los Angeles:

> A patient walked into her doctor's office. She had taken the medicine he had prescribed for her earache. She said there was some good news and some bad news. The good news was the medicine had worked. The doctor was pleased, but wanted to know the bad news.
>
> "It tasted awful!" she complained.
>
> The doctor couldn't bring himself to tell her that he had prescribed her ear drops.

This crazy story actually happened to Grossan. Let's take a moment and think about this in the context of listening. The patient was lucky that ingesting the ear drops didn't affect her negatively, but had she listened to her doctor she might have saved herself the shock of tasting that nasty medicine. When we listen to others we know exactly what they need.

#2. Feel the Sting

It was 2:00 a.m. My dad woke me up and said "Aaron, Zeke is trying to call you, you need to call him." I called Zeke (who is my best friend), and he said "Aaron, my brother James died tonight in a motorcycle accident." I was speechless. I had no words for him except to say that I was so sorry. James was the oldest brother; he was a pilot, a friend; and for me he was like my second brother. I remember spending many weekends sleeping over at their house when we were young, with James cracking jokes and sliding down the stairs in sleeping bags.

For me this accident was the closest person I had ever known to pass away. I went over the next morning to my friend Zeke's house and just hugged him, and we cried together. There was nothing that I could say that would make him feel better. I knew we both were feeling the pain. I remember sitting there for twenty minutes, not saying anything. Zeke later told me how much it meant to him that I was just there to listen to him and be with him. This heartbreaking experience showed me that sometimes the best way to care for someone is to just feel the sting with them. This is a moment in both of our lives that we will remember forever and taught me a very valuable lesson about listening.

One thing I learned was that my best friend did not need words of sympathy or a card from a store. He needed my empathy. Here's the distinction: Sympathy is feeling sorry for someone. Empathy is feeling with someone.

I FEEL YOUR PAIN
As Saint Paul wrote in his letter to the Romans, we do best when we "Rejoice with those who rejoice, weep with those who weep."

Empathy should help you feel the pain of others, without being controlled by it. This will help you understand the hurt people are going through. It will show you the pain they are going through and help you offer solutions.

#3. Preview the Solution
Maybe you've heard this advice for speakers. If not, you are in for a real treat. I'll put these words of wisdom in caps for emphasis:

TELL THEM WHAT YOU ARE GOING TO TELL THEM.
TELL THEM.
THEN TELL THEM WHAT YOU TOLD THEM.

Your audience is hoping you will take them on a journey and that you know where you are going.

At this early point in your speech you are trying to do two things: First, you are reminding them of the specific problem they are facing. Second, you are previewing your plan for helping them.

If this sounds complicated, it's not. Here is how you might say it in a talk, in just three sentences:

> This year, if we don't hit our sales goal of five million dollars, we will face layoffs and will lose some key people. We can't let that happen. I'm about to show you how we can, first, get back on track with our sales calls; second, exceed our sales goal; and third, have a lot of fun along the way.

I want you to really get how important this concept is. Previewing your solution like this is powerful after you have made it clear that you understand their pain. Telling them what you are going to tell them will help make you into a super speaker. To accomplish this, all you need is some strategic communication with key audience members before you craft your talk. Asking good questions is magic. Albert Einstein, who may have been the brightest thinker of the last century, said, "It is not that I'm so smart. But I stay with the questions much longer."

Dig into the questions before you provide the audience with your answers. Put a spotlight on their pain before you get to your solution. By listening to their pain, you are paving the way for your presentation to feel relevant, helpful, and important. You should never jump into your solution points before you have identified their problem and reminded them of their struggle.

The more deeply you listen to your audience, the better at connecting and communicating you will be.

We talk, talk, talk, talk, but I think 82.7 percent of how we communicate is how we first listen. Fine, I made up that stat, but you get the point.

I saw a funny comic strip of a guy and girl on their first date. The guy's thought bubble was: *Shoot, I'm not talking, she must think I'm boring, this date will go nowhere.* But the girl's thought bubble was: *Wow! He listens to me and hears what I have to say. I love him.* When we listen, we are communicating to someone that we love them and care about them. I urge you to love and care about your audience. They will feel it.

In the next chapter I'll share the secret to building the main part of your talk. Before we move on, take a moment to review these tools and add one or two takeaways from this chapter.

> *Most people won't change until the pain of where they are exceeds the pain of change.*
> **—DAVE RAMSEY,** *New York Times* **best-selling author**

TOOLS FOR YOUR TALK

- Listen before you speak.
- Ask questions to uncover pain points.
- Empathize with your audience before advising.

My personal takeaway:

_____

_____

_____

_____

POWER POINT: A STUNNING SYMBOL

The Chinese symbol for "listening" has multiple parts. To listen at the most powerful level, you must be fully present to hear, feel, and understand another person.

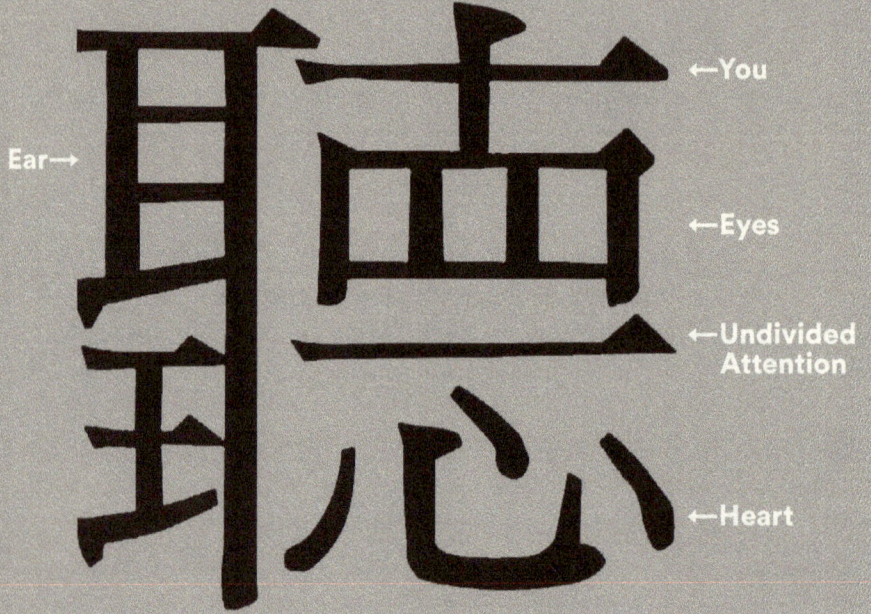

CHAPTER 3
EMPOWER THEM TO WIN

> *Rather than wishing for change,*
> *you first must be prepared to change.*
> **—CATHERINE PULSIFER, Author,**
> *Change Your Life: Successful People Who Did (Why Not You?)*

In 1980, Kareem Abdul Jabbar, the captain of the Los Angeles Lakers, was injured. It looked like the Lakers had no shot at winning the NBA championship. But this is a book about how to Speak Like Magic. So, enter Earvin "Magic" Johnson.

When the Lakers hopped onto their plane to head out to play game five of the NBA championship against the 76ers, there was one thing that looked different to the team and coaches. No Kareem. Kareem always sat in the same place on the team plane: Seat 1A. Even when the Laker center was sick, no one ever sat there, because it was Kareem's seat. Everybody respected the sign posted there: "Don't sit in my seat. I'm Kareem."

That day, Magic sat in Kareem's seat. He gave a little wink to the coach and said, "I'm Kareem."

Magic stepped up as their leader. He showed his team that he could do it, even though he was just a twenty-year-old rookie. Magic Johnson's greatest feat was not the forty-two points or the fifteen rebounds he put up that day, but empowering his team to believe that he was their leader. The Lakers needed someone to lead them, and Magic Johnson did just that. He first listened to his team and realized what they needed, then he stepped onto the court and delivered. Just as Magic took the seat, as the speaker you need to take the stage.

The Lakers went on to win the NBA championship, and Magic Johnson won the MVP award that same year in 1980. Magic Johnson's story of stepping into the leadership role is a great example of the magic of empowering your team, audience, group, attendees, and listeners to win!

But here's the point of this chapter: You are *the leader,* not the hero. Magic Johnson is one of the best passers in the history of professional basketball. He was always assisting his teammates on their way to five championships.

If your presentation is all about your audience, that makes them the hero. You are the one who empowers. You're the passer, the assist, the sidekick.

This reminds me of one of my favorite childhood movies: *Sky High.* The main character, Will, is attending a high school for teenagers with superpowers—but although his parents have superpowers, he actually doesn't have any. Learning this, the coach assigns Will to "Hero Support"—a sidekick. At the beginning of the film the sidekick is seen as weak and helpless, but the sidekicks become the real heroes of this story, because they empower the hero to win.

YOU ARE THE HERO'S SUPPORT

As a speaker, your audience is made up of heroes, and your job is to help them defeat evil. The "evil" is the problem or pain that you identified in the previous chapter. Treat your audience like heroes, not sidekicks. It's your speech. But remember, it's their story. And you are helping them achieve victory.

That means it's time to help them face the pain you discovered in the previous chapter head on.

In my family, when we have arguments or issues that arise, we try not to sweep things under the rug, but instead we face the problem head on, and we get things solved. There is going to be pain, but really it allows our family to win, because after we discuss the given situation, we can move on.

Now it's time to share your wisdom and your strengths with your audience.

This is the time for you to bring value and expertise to your listeners. Here is another metaphor: think of yourself as the doctor and your audience as your patients. You know exactly what they need to solve their problem and succeed. Your job is to share this with them and help empower them toward recovery and regained health. For some groups this might be closing a deal. For another audience it might be building a house for homeless people in the community. But the principle remains: You are assisting them in solving a problem.

But here's a problem many presenters face. To empower others, you must first feel empowered yourself. I invite you to look inward, build that confidence inside yourself, and let that grow and take root so you can then empower others to win. If you struggle with empowering yourself, I suggest you examine the way you speak to yourself.

EMPOWER YOURSELF BEFORE YOU EMPOWER YOUR AUDIENCE

What have you been saying to yourself before you speak to others?

- I can't do this.
- They won't care about what I have to say.
- I'm not qualified to speak to this group.
- What if I forget what to say?
- I am afraid they won't like me or my message.

Would you ever say things like this to another speaker before they stepped in front of their audience? "You can't do this." "You're not qualified." Of course you wouldn't! You would offer them supportive words of encouragement: "You can do this." "You're going to inspire them." Now, give yourself the same kind of support:

- I can do this!
- I want to make this presentation, and I'm grateful for the opportunity.
- They will feel inspired by what I have to share.
- This will help me grow personally and professionally.
- I want to help others succeed.
- This is going to be fun.

Say these words out loud—even if you don't (yet) believe them. Jay Mincks, the senior vice president of Insperity, likes to say: "What you say is what you get." Multiple studies have shown how speaking confidently to yourself boosts your level of success.

Once you give yourself the empowerment to achieve what you need to do, it is time to help empower others so that they will win as well.

HERE'S HOW TO EMPOWER YOUR AUDIENCE TO WIN
Propose a simple remedy for solving what's wrong. Don't be vague. Outline steps for solving the problem. Move your audience from information to transformation. How? By first reminding them of the wonderful experience they will have when they reach their goals, then showing them exactly how they can get there. You want to keep your speech clear and concise. Here are the STEPS you need to know as you deliver your plan of empowerment.

SPECIFIC

Tell them precisely what to do to overcome the pain you identified in the previous phase. If the solution is losing weight, have your listeners determine exactly how much weight they should lose. "Get in shape" is too vague. "Lose twenty pounds by eating no more than two thousand calories a day and staying away from sugar and fatty foods. Also, make a plan to run one mile around your block six days a week."

THREE

There is something truly magical about the power of three! Ever notice that? Past, present, future. Beginning, middle, end. Blood, sweat, tears. Stop, look, listen. I came, I saw, I conquered. You get the idea. Make sure your audience is not overloaded with action steps. Hit them with three steps.

EASY TO REMEMBER

Make your speech memorable by making your solution steps simple, clear, and easy to remember (see that three?). That old saying is true: "Less is more." Here are examples of steps you could present in an easy-to-retain way:

Alliteration: 1. Count (calories). **2.** Cook (at home). **3.** Control (carbs).

Acronyms: WIN: Write down goals. Invest in coaching. Now begin.

ABCs: Apply for jobs. Be early to interviews (not too early, per my dad, the owner of Jason Best Staffing). Check back with the employer.

PRACTICAL

You must offer your audience actionable steps. If you say "Do better," that sounds good but gives your listeners nothing to actually do. Identify concrete next steps.

> Examples: This is good: Strengthen your heart by increasing your heart rate regularly with aerobic exercise. This is better: Take a brisk walk every morning before breakfast for twenty minutes.
>
> **STRATEGIC**
> Don't give your audience "busy work." Your steps must be the key actions they need to take to get what they need. You are providing the cure for their disease. If you met someone who was bitten by a rattlesnake, you wouldn't offer them a long lecture on the history of rattlers. You would clearly give them a blueprint of what to do right away.
>
> Examples: You have been bitten by a rattlesnake! **1.** Call 911. **2.** Get medical attention. **3.** Take the medication.

This phase of your speech is the actual content of your message. Your goal here is to tell your participants exactly what they need to know to get what they want. If you are giving a thirty-minute talk, this section could easily fill fifteen minutes. It's the 1, 2, 3 steps section, the main body of your presentation. Do you know what is far more important than using PowerPoint slides in your presentation? Making powerful points that empower your audience to win. Guide them to the awesome outcome you promised at the end of the listen phase. Give them the plan they need to help them attain victory. Be their Yoda.

Let's review. So far in your speech, you have personalized your message, identified where your audience is hurting, and described exactly what they need to do to cross the finish line to win. But the next step is a powerful secret. Most speakers skip it. But it's critical that you use it to deliver an amazing message. I'll unpack it for you in the next chapter. But before I reveal it, take a moment to note your big takeaway lesson from this chapter.

TOOLS FOR YOUR TALK
It's as easy as A, B, C...

- Offer the **A**nswer.
- Provide the **B**lueprint.
- Give then the **C**lear steps.

My personal takeaway:

_____

_____

_____

_____

POWER POINT: COMMUNICATING WITH INTERPERSONAL IMPACT

Most of this book is about preparing and presenting a great public talk. That's why they call it "public speaking." But much of communication is interpersonal (one on one). Notice that texting is near the bottom of the power pyramid!

Sharing a meal in person
Face-to-face meeting
Handwritten note
FaceTime/Zoom
Phone convos
Social media
Texting
Email

CHAPTER 4

AUTHORIZE THEM TO MOVE FORWARD

> *The degree to which you as a leader believe in your people and communicate that belief can play a huge role in unlocking their potential and getting the most out of your team.*
> **—DANIEL HARVEY, Building Champions**

Serena Williams is a world champion tennis player. She has won twenty-three grand slam titles. The career of this incredible athlete offers wisdom for us. In 2010, after sustaining a foot injury, Serena began losing matches. Suddenly her bright future in tennis was in doubt.

But Serena gave herself permission to start all over again.

Once she regained her health, she made the difficult decision to stop being coached by her dad. She found a new coach: Patrick Mouratoglou. This move revitalized her game. She developed new techniques and a powerful mind-set and started dominating once again. Serena won her next nineteen matches. She won at Wimbledon and the US

Open, and she earned a gold medal at the 2012 Summer Olympic Games, where she defeated Maria Sharapova.

It was a difficult decision for Serena to make such a big change after having her dad as her coach for most of her career. Serena had to give herself permission to make this tremendous move.
To help your listeners get into gear, authorize them to move forward and make the changes they need to make to implement your plan of action.

I will share another secret with you. *Stories can help you help them.* When you share stories of forward motion, you give your audience rocket fuel for growth.

Whether you are telling a story about a historical person, a personal experience, or making up a story, a story—like the Serena Williams story—can help you persuade your listeners to decide to move forward and succeed.

TEN TIPS FOR TELLING IMPACTFUL STORIES

1. Don't just retell a tale. Relive it. Bring it to life!
2. Your story must have one main character.
3. Be sure to set up your story with a clear beginning.
4. Remember: Who? What? Where? When?
5. If your story has no conflict, you have no story.
6. Make sure your story has an unexpected twist or change.
7. Stay on the path. (Avoid rabbit holes.)
8. Pause for dramatic effect. Silence is loud.
9. Wrap up your tale with a clear ending.
10. The best stories have a single big takeaway.

By helping your listeners say yes to moving forward, you will authorize them to take action, and you are preparing them for the big finale of your talk. How do you help them say yes? There are three keys to moving people forward during your presentation. They are quite magical. This part of your presentation is like a pep talk.

Pep talks (which, by the way, according to Theidioms.com, go back to 1926) are aimed at activating people to step into personal achievement. Merriam-Webster defines a pep talk as a "brief, intense, and emotional talk designed to influence or encourage an audience."

In his article for the *Harvard Business Review*, "The Science of Pep Talks," Daniel McGinn describes how four-star general Stanley McChrystal would craft his pep talk for young soldiers. McChrystal would explain:

- Here's what I'm asking you to do.
- Here's why it's important.
- Here's why I know you can do it.
- Now, let's go and do it.

One of my favorite movies is the classic feel-good film *Rudy*. My family watched this inspirational film the Friday night before the first Notre Dame football game. It got me pumped. It made me want to take the field in my own life. It made me want to go out and do it. Though I became a magician and not a football player, the lesson for me was the same. *I must move forward.*

There is a key moment in *Rudy* when Rudy Ruettiger is confronted by his boss, whose name is Fortune. (It's almost like the screenwriter is reminding us of the classic Latin proverb: "Fortune favors the bold.") Fortune gives Rudy a very direct pep talk and reminds him to not give up, but to go for it. This comes at a critical time in Rudy's story. He is ready to quit and give up his dream of playing football for Notre Dame.

Fortune tells the young man: "I guarantee a week won't go by in your life you won't regret walking out, letting them get the best of you. Do you hear me clear enough?"

Rudy gets the message. Fortune reminds him that he is indeed "a somebody" and that he needs to step back into the arena.

This part of your speech is like a mini message inside of your larger message. It may last only two to three minutes, but it is critical. It's about sending your group into game-time mode. I like the acronym PEP. It stands for: permission, encourage, and pledge.

Give your audience...

_P_ermission to win

_E_ncourage them to "fail forward."

And invite them to make a...
_P_ledge.

Let's dig into each part of PEP together:

Give your audience permission to **win.**

What do people secretly hope you will give them?

We are all waiting for it. Permission! Approval! The green light! Real magic happens when you motivate your listeners to give themselves permission to do what they need to do. Position yourself as their coach. You are championing their success.

This happened for me personally in high school in an unexpected way.

It was 9 a.m., and it was the end of my sophomore year of high school. I had just finished a grueling two-hour workout on top of a two-hour high school football practice. I was exhausted—and I felt that I wasn't living up to my potential. My career path as a magician had begun to take shape, and I needed to decide between magic and football. I knew that I didn't want to be the guy who told people that I used to do magic; I wanted to be the person who lived up to his dreams. My coach stood across from me, arms crossed, as I began to explain to him that I wanted to be a professional magician.

He looked at me as if I told him that I'd totaled his brand-new red Ferrari. I will never forget his words: "Aaron, if you stop playing football and do this little magic thing you will regret this for the rest of your life."

Well, I have never regretted my decision—never, not once. Magic and speaking have given me the life I always wanted, and I have been so blessed by many amazing people who have encouraged me. But this was a critical moment in my life, because his perspective was so different from mine: it actually motivated me to commit fully to my dream. His words made it so clear that we were talking about two different dreams: his for me, and mine for me.

Right then, I gave myself permission to succeed. I left behind the dream my coach had for me and instead developed my dream and my passion. If my coach ever reads this book, I want to thank him. This conversation gave me permission to live out my dreams and succeed on my own terms.

Here's the best part: Coach Henderson ultimately *affirmed me.* Two years later, he hired me to perform my magic at the high school football banquet! This made me very happy, and I gratefully accepted the gig.

Your role as an inspiring speaker is to affirm your audience—to give them the go-ahead. Coach H did this when he hired me. You can do it by firing *up* your audience.

Human beings tend to make changes to prove someone else either right or wrong. As a communicator, during this part of your six-part speech sequence, get this message across to your listeners:

ADVANCE TO GO.

Encourage them to fail forward.

Nearly every great achievement has been connected to some kind of failure. Achievement happens for people who ignore the "Negative Nellies" and listen to the "Positive Pauls" around them. For some people, you may be the first positive reinforcing voice they have heard in a long time. Remind the individuals in your audience to surround themselves with people—like you—who will build them up.

Here's an exercise you can have an audience experience. Give them sticky notes and have them write down just one word for something that they were afraid of ten years ago that feels harmless to them now. Next, have them take a separate sticky note and write down one word indicating something they are afraid of today. Invite them to place that note in their pocket, take it back home, and seal it in an envelope marked "To be opened [ten years from today's date]." You get the point (and so will they): most of the things we fear today will melt away in time.

But you can encourage people to deal with fear by taking action now.

Invite them to make a pledge.

Tell your attendees to be like rubber bands, not candy canes.

When a rubber band is stretched, it grows—it is flexible. But try to stretch a candy cane? It will snap and shatter into a bunch of pieces.

Have you ever heard of the Boys & Girls Club? It started off as "The Dashaway Club" in the late 1800s. In 1880, Mary Stuart Hall—the first female lawyer in the state of Connecticut—made a pledge. She was committed to proving that tough street kids could, if given the opportunity, become positive citizens. She kept her promise and worked with children until her death in 1927. The "Good Will Boys Club" continues today as the Boys & Girls Club.

This organization now serves over four million kids and teens every year. Just as Mary Stuart Hall pledged to help change the lives of children, you can authorize your audience to make a powerful pledge.

The difference between a wish and a pledge is simple: A wish is a hope, a dream. A pledge is an intention to act and succeed. This part of your presentation is all about getting your audience to say yes to their success.

HERE ARE THREE OTHER "P" WORDS THAT HOLD YOUR LISTENERS BACK:
Paralysis: Your audience probably feels stuck. Your mission? Help them get unstuck and feel the freedom to move. This is an important point. Your goal is not to get them into a thinking or analytical mode. As businessman and self-help author W. Clement Stone said, "Thinking will not overcome fear, but action will."

Perfectionism: This is a killer. Don't let your group fall into this trap. During your pep talk, you want to remind them that it's all about progress, not perfection. It's much easier to steer a car that's moving than one that's parked.

Procrastination: Do you like the stars of *Shark Tank*? I like this show a lot. Daymond John, one of the sharks on the show, says: "Don't wait for the 'perfect time'; you will wait forever. Always take advantage of the time that you're given."

Often our obstacles are imaginary. By giving your audience permission, authorizing them to make change, you may be helping them overcome their biggest barrier. Give yourself permission to stop getting ready and just do it. You don't have to be the "right age." If you are breathing, go for it.

As of this writing, I'm twenty-one, and I could have talked myself out of writing this book. *How can you possibly write a book? You're too young.* But I talked myself into writing it. I just sat down and did it. I claimed authority in my life and my business and made it happen. Maybe you are middle-aged. Well, no problem. Don't have a midlife crisis; create a midlife success story instead. And if you are in your upper years, that's great. The best is yet to come—if you decide to live that way.

As a communicator, you need to keep this important reality in mind: You can't change anybody; however, *you can inspire them to make a change*. And you can say, with faith: I believe you can do it. Our next secret will enable you to prove to your audience that they can do just that. But first, take a moment to jot down your biggest lesson from this chapter.

TOOLS FOR YOUR TALK

- Insert a three-minute positive pep talk into your speech.
- Help your audience get out of fear and into gear.
- Give your group the green light to GO.

My personal takeaway:

_____

_____

_____

_____

POWER POINT: SPEAKING OF "AUTHORIZING" OTHERS TO WIN

Which of these famous authors persisted and failed forward until he/she became a successful author?

This writer was rejected numerous times by publishers. The writer was broke and had to work a second job. Everyone told the writer to stop writing and just give up.

Who was it?

> J. K. Rowling
> Stephen King
> Jack Canfield
> Mark Twain

(Flip upside down for the answer.)

(Answer: All four of them)

CHAPTER 5
SHOW THEM IT WORKS

> **❝**
> *Let me show you how it's done...Loser!*
> **—BABE RUTH**
> **❞**

Did you read that quotation? I'm just making sure you are paying attention.

The legendary Babe Ruth was the greatest home run hitter of his day. And while I don't want you to call people "losers," I want you to know that your message will hit a home run when you follow my PLEASE sequence. We are now on step five. You have spent several minutes giving your audience permission to move forward with your blueprint; now it's time to *show them* that your three steps will work for them.

Babe Ruth could send a baseball over the outfield fence with his bat. But I want to tell you about another superstar with a great name who launched into flight herself. Sally Ride (talk about a perfect name for an astronaut) was the first American woman to fly into space. Later she became the founder of Sally Ride Science. Here's what Sally Ride had to say about the importance of showing others what could be done: "Young girls need to see role models, so they can picture themselves doing those jobs someday. You can't be what you can't see."

Ride was inducted into the Astronaut Hall of Fame. And up until her death in 2012, Sally Ride was all about showing girls (and boys) what was possible. She started NASA's EarthKAM project to help young people see and study photos of planet Earth using a camera set up on the International Space Station.

To deliver a speech that launches your audience upward, you need to show them what they can accomplish by following your plan. Killer-good speakers paint word pictures. There are many ways to do this. I'm going to give you three ways to show them the magic during this phase of your speech.

As you are approaching the powerful end of your presentation, and before you urge your listeners to take action, you must give them a "3-D" experience that will showcase your plan in action. Here are your 3-D's:

1. **Display the before and after.**
2. **Document the proof.**
3. **Demonstrate that they can experience the results.**

This is a *powerful* component of your speech. Don't you dare skip it.

Too many speakers rush through their main points, wrap up abruptly, and say, "Well, thanks for having me here. I'll be around at the back if you have questions."

No. Don't do this. You are not done yet. You must show them that following your plan will lead to solving the problem you addressed in step two (Listen to Their Pain). Have them see the before-and-after effect.

A perfect example of this is Chip and Joanna Gaines, the superstars of *Fixer Upper* on HGTV and their Magnolia Network empire. This dynamic duo helps couples find and fix up run-down homes on a budget and then makes them look amazing inside and out. They do a marvelous job of *displaying* the before and after by *documenting* the change process with photos and video. Then they reveal the results to the couple and those watching at home.

The first step may be the couple choosing a house they like from options in their desired area, or they may already have a house that needs TLC. Then Chip and Joanna describe how they can transform the house to bring forth the couple's vision.

The couple meets with Joanna to talk about interior design choices. Comical Chip comes in for demolition day, bashing out problematic walls, cupboards, plumbing fixtures, and so on, and gets it all set up for the couple so they can see the "good bones" of the house. The next step is the renovation, with Chip leading construction while Joanna works more on the interior design. During these phases, Chip and Joanna *document* their work for both the couple and their audience at home.

One real genius feature of this show is how the Gaineses present the before and after on the big day—that is, the big reveal, when the couple gets to see the transformed house for the first time. The house is concealed behind a billboard-size image of the house as it was before. (For viewers, there are clips of the "pain point" elements, a reminder of all they had agreed had to be changed.) Joanna and Chip pull apart the two sides of the house as it was, revealing the newly transformed home.

Reveal day brings out the biggest emotions from the couples: some cry, some laugh, but most important are the wide-eyed gasp, the hands to their faces, and those beaming smiles. Reactions that can't help but make you smile too.

Notice how Chip and Joanna Gaines use the amazing strategies of *display, document, and demonstrate* to impact their homeowners. You can tap into these powers as you Speak Like Magic.

SEEING THE SOLUTION IS POWERFUL

A friend of mine was featured on one of the Proactiv acne treatment commercials. Have you watched these? Acne is a condition that approximately fifty million Americans—young (and older)—struggle to overcome. Proactiv generated more than $2 billion in 2016. Proactiv commercials show regular people (and celebrities like Justin Bieber, Katy Perry, and Jessica Simpson) before and after using Proactiv. Before-and-after pictures are a major factor in the success of Proactiv.

Think of the problem you are solving as pimples. Show them how your plan makes zits (low sales, bad health, lack of direction) disappear. Make sure you employ the power of this strategy as you Speak Like Magic. How? *Display* visual slides or video clips that show them what happens when they do (or don't) follow your plan.

Document the proof.

One of General Colin Powell's favorite sayings is just four words long:

It can be done!

This is the conviction you want your audience to feel at this point in your speech. To help them get there, you should document—that is, prove to them—that your action plan works. Here are some ways you can show them that your message points are rock solid and will bring them tremendous satisfaction—if they act on them.

- Use statistics to prove your point. Heads up: Sprinkle in just a few powerful stats. Remember that facts tell, but stories sell.
- Share success stories of others (just like your listeners) who have implemented what you are suggesting. Better yet, if possible, have live (or video recorded) stories of people who have

put your solution steps into action.
- Reference studies confirming that your plan works. (Just be sure to keep it lively, not static.)
- Use slides and videos that illustrate the effectiveness of what you are recommending.

Consider tapping into what I call "the tale of two testimonies." This is powerful! You have one person share what happened when they didn't follow your suggested plan (ongoing pain). The other shares what happened when they did implement your solution (satisfaction).

Here's the purpose of this phase of your presentation: You want your audience to believe that what they have seen will also work for *them*—that they will experience positive results and get what they desire.

Have you ever purchased a George Foreman grill, Mike Lindell's My Pillow, or one of dozens of other celebrity-branded products sold via infomercials? Why do these commercial pitches work so well? It's simple: They tap into the magic power of demonstration.

The people in the demo were in some kind of pain before they tried this product. Now they are so much better off. This could be you!

Human beings are skeptical. Is this going to work for me? Consider your audience skeptical until you have convinced them. Take the advice of the late great drummer and lyricist of Rush, Neil Peart, who wrote: "Show me, don't tell me."

Display the before and after. Visuals will aid you in this part of your speech. Hey, that's why they are called visual aids.

ELEVEN GREAT VISUAL AIDS
Here are eleven of my favorite visual aids. Choose the visuals that you feel most comfortable using. Most important, use the technology (photos, videos, on-stage demonstrations, testimonials, and so on)

that will best show the audience that your proposed solution really, truly, absolutely works.

- PowerPoint. When done right, i.e. sparingly, it can be very effective. Just avoid "Death by PowerPoint."
- Audience participation. Bring attendees right on the stage with you. If you are giving a virtual presentation, call on individuals by name and ask for their involvement.
- Funny photos.
- Short video clips.
- Magic tricks. And guess what? Visit my website, AaronOBrien.com, and learn a trick you can do for free.
- Flip charts.
- Printed handouts.
- On-screen game shows or trivia contests that reinforce your messaging.
- Real-time surveys via texting.
- Customized apps accessible by attendees' smartphones.
- *Prizes.*

Engage the eyes of your audience so they see that your message points are valid. Visual aids work if you work them.

Remember that you are the most important visual aid. Few things are as powerful to humans as seeing the human face and hearing the human voice. So light yourself on fire with enthusiasm.

Finally, make sure your visual aids are dynamic, not static. They call movies "motion pictures" for a reason. You need to be moving, smiling, raising or lowering your voice, getting closer to attendees, engaging, and re-engaging them. Too many speakers rely on static visual aids, like boring slides or overly long videos.

You know the expression "Death by PowerPoint"? Don't be that speaker who recites all the text on every slide. Any text should be brief, so your audience can quickly take it in as you expand on it with further thoughts and stories. Don't let your visual aids be passive; make your visual aids dynamic.

This is also the part of your presentation where you warn your audience: Here's what will happen if you do not follow this plan. Remind them of the same pain you identified in step two (Listen to Their Pain).

I am about to show you how to wrap up your talk in a magical way. But first, some homework for you: Take a second to make note of your biggest takeaway(s) from this chapter.

TOOLS FOR YOUR TALK

- How will you *show them* that your pain reliever works?
- What is your *before* and *after* visual?
- Can you create a way for them to experience the results?

My personal takeaway:

_____

_____

_____

_____

POWER POINT: A VISUAL PERSPECTIVE CHANGER...

Read this poem by "A. O.," a ten-year-old British student. She calls the poem "Dyslexia." You can read it both forward and backward. Think of how this shows the power of changing your point of view!

DYSLEXIA

I am stupid
Nobody would ever say
I have a talent for words

I was meant to be great
That is wrong
I am a failure

Nobody could ever convince me to think that
I can make it in life

Now read it from the bottom up!

CHAPTER 6
ENCOURAGE THEM TO GO FOR IT

> *If you can't fly then run, if you can't run then walk, if you can't walk then crawl, but whatever you do, you have to keep moving forward.*
> **—MARTIN LUTHER KING JR.**

Indra Nooyi is an inspiring Indian American business leader. She was the CEO for PepsiCo from 2006 to 2018. During her tenure, PepsiCo's annual revenues soared from $35 billion to $64 billion.

When she visited India, many people thanked Indra's mother for encouraging her to become the woman she became. This touched Indra in a powerful way. Rather than developing an ego from the praise she and her mother received, she moved into action.

Seeing how people thanked her mom meant so much that she decided to bring this type of affirmation to others. She wrote four hundred letters to the parents of her senior executives. Many of these parents responded to Nooyi to thank her. Nooyi is a model of the power of encouragement.

The word "encourage" means the act of giving *strength or heart* to another. In this chapter, I will show you how to conclude your speech in a way that has your audience ready to go for it. But first, let's stop for a moment. Are you paying attention? I want you to really hear me on this.

The purpose of your speech is not to impress them, but to press them to take action. Take a look at this famous story of two speakers. And choose to be Demosthenes in your own speaking.

BE DEMOSTHENES

David Ogilvy was a legendary advertising man. In his book *Ogilvy on Advertising*, he described the key difference between two ancient Greek speakers: Demosthenes and Aeschines:

When Aeschines spoke, the gatherers said, "How well he speaks."

But when Demosthenes spoke, they said, "Let us march!"

You want to be Demosthenes. The ultimate aim of your speech is to encourage your audience to go for it. Speaking like magic means motivating people to get up and take action. The goal is not to have people say, "Oh, she was interesting to listen to." No. It's all about moving people to take the medicine you have prescribed for them. The goal is to get them off their butts and into gear to do what you have laid out for them to do.

James Allen was one of the great inspirational writers of all time, and possibly the originator of what became the self-help movement. In his tremendous book *As a Man Thinketh*, he wrote:

"The will to do comes from the knowledge that we can do."

That verb, can, provides the perfect acronym (have you kept track of how many acronyms we have learned?) for this powerful sixth step of PLEAS<u>E</u>: *Encourage them to go for it.* Here's how: Let them know they CAN experience the change you are recommending. CAN stands for:

1. Concentration
2. Action
3. Now!

This part of your speech is your grand finale. It may only last about two minutes, but it's vital to your success as a speaker.

Let's look at each part.

1. Concentration

My first mentor gave me a bit of classic advice: Keep It Simple, Stupid. It has helped me (and so many others) through life and is particularly good advice for delivering focused presentations.

This phrase has helped me remember to keep my speech simple. Do not ramble on with facts or stats; instead, tell them precisely what to go out and do.

Dave Ramsey, who has been helping people all around the world get out of debt for years, created a system he calls "the baby steps." Picture a baby who is still mastering the skill of walking. Total focus, right? Unwavering purpose. What a great picture of concentration. A baby's first steps are small, but each one is a move in the right direction.

2. Action

You must understand what action means. You are not merely flattering them—"Hey, you have been a great crowd." You are doing something way more important. You are encouraging them to take action.

Here are five ways you can inspire your audience to take action:

1. **Remind them that they are not alone in saying yes to your action plan.** We don't accomplish much in this world by ourselves. People love to feel that they are part of a community that is committed to winning together.
2. **Share a plan for being accountable.** This might be an exercise in which each attendee writes a postcard addressed to themself, stating what they plan to do within the next week, and places a stamp on it. Then, guess what? You mail these to them a week later. It's powerful.
3. **Have participants sign a physical or virtual pledge.** The act of doing this does two great things. It calls for personal commitment. And it creates a spirit of unity. One of the most powerful abilities is accountability.
4. **Get them to move.** This might sound silly, but it sends an important signal. Here's what you do: Invite audience members to do something right where they are. This might be raising their hands, changing seats, coming to the front of the room, saying something to the attendee next to them. Something that gets them moving.
5. **Ask for an out-loud verbal commitment.** "All in favor of taking action on steps 1, 2, and 3, say 'I'm in.'"

Now!

Some of the most powerful speeches of all time aren't really speeches—they are thirty- to sixty-second commercials. We can learn something super-powerful from them. What makes them so effective? One word: urgency. You've seen and heard these. "Sale ends Sunday!" "Limited supplies on hand." "Only ten left in stock!" What these ad creators understand is the critical importance of getting people to take action today, now, immediately.

Remember: It's not just what you make them think (or feel); it's what you inspire them to do.

Zig Ziglar was one of the most motivational speakers of all time. He said, "You don't have to be great to start, but you do have to start to be great."

This is the final push of your speech. Be bold. Be like the man who invited his listeners to come to the edge…

> "Come to the edge," he said.
>
> "We can't! We're afraid!" they responded.
>
> "Come to the edge," he said.
>
> "We can't! We will fall!" they responded.
>
> "Come to the edge," he said.
>
> And so they came.
>
> And he pushed them.
>
> And they flew.
>
> **—GUILLAUME APOLLINAIRE**

REWIND AND REVIEW

Your mission as a speaker is to leave your audience knowing exactly what they need to do and feeling inspired to do it. This will be impossible if you go off on bunny trails, stray from your main points, or allow your group to simply nod their heads and think, That was good. I agree with that.

Big Tip: At this point in your speech, briefly review what you have already covered. Remind your listeners of their big pain point. Then quickly review the specific steps you shared for solving that problem.

It might sound like this:

"Let's review what we talked about today. Some people in this room will not be here next year if we don't hit our sales goal. We can't let that happen. So here's the plan we need to concentrate on: (1) Get back on track with our *customer calls*, (2) exceed our sales goal, and (3) *pull together as a team to get it done. You have seen how this works. Now, who's ready to go for it?*

Just as you want to review the main points of your talk at the end of your speech, let's take a moment to review our six secrets. As you prepare and deliver your talk, remember to PLEASE your audience by following this sequence:

- Personalize your message for them.
- Listen to their pain.
- Empower them to win.
- Authorize them to move forward.
- Show them it works.
- Encourage them to go for it.

Follow these secrets, in the order you just learned, and you will wow them. And that's the real magic: getting your message across to the hearts and minds of your audience.

I am going to give you a "cheat sheet" coming up. But first, I want to encourage you to go for it and implement these ideas. Answer these questions for yourself as *you* begin to Speak Like Magic.

TOOLS FOR YOUR TALK

- How can you simplify your ending so they can *concentrate* on what to do?
- What will you say that will inspire them to take *action*?
- How will you get them to see the urgency of acting *now*?

My personal takeaway:

_____

_____

_____

_____

_____

BONUS CHAPTER

TEN TIPS FOR HOW TO SPEAK LIKE MAGIC IN VIRTUAL MEETINGS

We have entered a new age of virtual meetings. Many people are having a hard time pivoting to these new platforms. Here are some strategies that will help you engage virtual audiences and be a better virtual speaker. Enjoy.

1. **Pick your platform and know your technology.** Choose a platform that is user-friendly and will allow you to see the people in your audience. This is why I highly recommend the Zoom platform. It's easy to learn. Most technical difficulties happen when the speaker is unfamiliar with the platform. Technology is only as good as the operator, so be sure you know how to handle exactly what you'll be using, to avoid fumbling and dead air. If you do not have the time to learn it all on your own, consider hiring a young college student to assist you. He or she will have you on screen in no time.

2. **Have great lighting so you can be seen.** This is huge. You do not need a massive studio setup, but do invest in some good lighting.

It's hard to connect with your participants if you are in the dark and they can't see you. Look at the video feed *before* you go into a meeting so you can see what you look like. Purchase a light that will illuminate you well. There are some great options via Amazon.com. Example: For about $150 you can purchase the Neewer Light and Stand Kit. If you *really* don't want to spend any money, at least frame your meeting so your face is lit by natural light from a window. *More on what they see:* Find a good space to set up. It should look clean and uncluttered. An organized bookcase or muted art can lend a touch of personality. Warning: A virtual background can be distracting (you're in a tropical paradise, and your audience members are stuck in their homes). Low production value will detract from your overall professionalism.

3. **Audio is key.** Consider investing in a good clip-on microphone so the audience can hear you. If they can't hear you speaking, there is no speech! This is simple: have your attendees give you a thumbs-up to verify that they can hear you. Do this before you start your presentation. You don't want to be two minutes into your speech and find out they haven't heard a word you've said.

4. **Capture attention at the beginning** and hold onto it. Virtual settings create a different set of challenges from live presentations. If an individual wants to close his or her screen and leave, they can. So be sure to grab your audience's attention at the beginning of your speech by asking a question, telling a joke, or sharing a compelling visual. (See Chapter 1 for more ideas. Personalization is powerful.) It's all about making and keeping connections. You may be speaking to fifty people, but look directly into your camera as if you are talking to a close friend.

5. **Use people's names.** With attendees' names displayed, it's as if everyone is wearing name tags. So you can and should address individuals by name. The virtual format makes many people feel disconnected. Use this as an opportunity to connect people to you—and to each other. The best way to remember names is to

actually look at your screen. (If you are on Zoom, go to gallery mode when speaking, so you can watch your audience.) You can place a sticky note with names at the top or side of your monitor for quick reference.

6. **Be dynamic!** Look into software like Open Broadcaster Software (OBS) or Ecamm (for Mac) that allows you to insert a slideshow or video into your program. Look for ways to enliven your presentation and keep people awake. We have all been in those boring Zoom meetings where one person is just talking on and on for an hour. Periodically have everyone stand up or do something to *keep the energy flowing.*

> **PRO TIP**
>
> Speaking to a company? Use a software product like OBS or ECAMM to incorporate your client's logo into your presentation. They will love it.

7. **Encourage questions.** This keeps people engaged. When you welcome their questions, people feel heard. And don't forget. You are the expert on your topic. People will want to hear your responses to the questions that come up in their minds during your speech.

8. **Build interactive elements into your talk.** People love to hear themselves. So give them a chance to share and participate (without losing control of the time). If you see people drifting, or distracted, stop talking. This will recapture their attention. Silence is strong. They will all look up to see what's happened. This is the perfect opportunity to re-engage them in your session. More ideas: trivia games, magic tricks, wine tasting.

9. **Focus on community.** We've all had to shift to virtual events, and this will remain the case, with many events becoming a

hybrid of digital *and* in-person attendance. People need human connection now more than ever. You can bring some wonderful community-building into your presentation. Example: Before the program, send your attendees a "discovery box" in the mail. This gets opened in real time by your participants *together* during your session. Keep the contents of the box a secret. This will build suspense prior to the meeting and maintain their interest during your time together. The key here is getting your attendees enjoying a *shared experience*.

10. **Remember that this is still a speech.** Even in a virtual setting, use the PLEASE six-secret sequence. Just as when you are giving an in-person message you want your audience to walk away at the end (closing their screens, that is) with solid takeaway value. Make sure you identify their pain, show them how to solve their problem, and tell them how to take action. Oh, and one more thing: Be sure to thank them for the privilege of presenting.

YOUR ONE-PAGE "CHEAT SHEET" SPEECH OUTLINE

This simple outline is based on our PLEASE sequence.
Here is a thirty-minute presentation example:

STEP 1: Personalize Your Message for Them *(two minutes)*
WHO are you talking to?

*Mention the organization or group.
*Refer to and thank several people by name.
*Use at least one "inside" phrase, acronym, or buzzword they know well.

STEP 2: Listen to Their Pain *(three minutes)*
WHY must they pay attention?

*Share why and how you understand where they are hurting—that is, the problem they face.
*Remind them of what is at stake if this is not solved!
*Let them know that you have a solution, and preview your three main points.

STEP 3: Empower Them to Win *(fifteen minutes)*
HOW will you help them?

*This is the body or main part of your presentation.
*Spend approximately five minutes on each of your three main points.
*Make it clear that if they follow these steps, your audience will succeed—that is, solve the problem.

STEP 4: Authorize Them to Move Forward *(three minutes)*
ARE they in?

*Insert your passionate pep talk here.
*Give them permission to get started.
*Invite them to accept your solution(s), and ask for a big YES.

STEP 5: Show Them It Works *(four minutes)*
WHAT is your proof?

*Have them see your solution in action. Example: The before and after.
*Demonstrate that they can get the same results.
*Provide a testimonial via an audience member or a video clip.

STEP 6: Encourage Them to Go for It *(three minutes)*
WILL they do it?

*Review your talking points—that is, their pain or problem and your three-part solution.
*Create a sense of urgency and a warning about not taking action.
*Tell them exactly what to *do*.

Wrap up briefly and thank them.

(YOUR NOTES FROM PRESENTATION)

STEP 1: WHO are you talking to?

___

___

STEP 2: WHY must they pay attention?

___

___

STEP 3: HOW will you help them?

___

___

STEP 4: ARE they in?

___

___

STEP 5: WHAT is your proof?

___

___

STEP 6: WILL they do it?

___

___

ACKNOWLEDGMENTS

I first and foremost want to thank God for all of the blessings he has provided me with.

I also want to thank my beautiful fiancée, Hailey, for all her love and dedication to me and what I do. Thank you for helping read all of the drafts and always supporting me. I'm so happy to have you in my life. I love you!

My whole career would not be where it is today if not for my parents, Tim and Melinda O'Brien. Thank you, Mom and Dad, for taking me down to the Magic Castle once a month so I could attend my meetings. This helped me grow tremendously. Also thank you for always loving me and telling me you were proud of me even though I was a magician.

Additionally, I want to thank my awesome brother, Shane, who may get annoyed by all my magic but still loves me the same. Love you man.

My magic career and this book would not be possible without my sweet and sincere grandparents. I love you both so much and thank you for always having me over for dinner. I'm so happy that you always made me perform a magic trick every time. It helped me grow and become more creative. Thanks, Trapper Dave, for all the fun we have and helping me build props.

Thank you to my uncles, Mike and Dan, and their wives, Susie and Karen, for always talking with me about my career and helping me achieve my dreams with your continued support. You both have blessed me so much in my life and career. I love our long talks on the phone and always look forward to telling you what is new with me.

I would also like to thank Adam Christing, for your continued support of my life and my career. Without your help and encouragement, this book would not exist. Thank you for helping me grow as a presenter, businessman, author, and person. And Barb Christing and Brian McElreath, you have made me feel so special being part of the *CleanComedians.com* family. Bang that gong, Brian! You are unstoppable.

Also huge thanks to my two best friends in the world, Zeke Lopez and Austin Janik. Zeke, thank you for letting me include the story about James. I hope that this book will be an honor to his memory. Thank you for always being there for me in the good and bad times. Love you bro! Austin, you are one of the best magicians I know and such a creative guy. I enjoy our late-night conversations about magic and pretty much anything. Thank you for always pushing me to be a better performer and businessman. Thanks again for helping me edit part of the book.

I want to acknowledge David Debranksy for showing me my very first magic trick when I was twelve. Little did you know that you were introducing me to the art and craft that would become my life's work.

Thanks to my Insperity friends, including the legendary Jay Mincks. Thanks to Karen Millard: you have been so supportive, and I appreciate our friendship. Richard and Dawn Rawson, I appreciate your wisdom and encouragement.

There is no way I could overlook Jim and Linda Johnson. I can never thank you enough for taking me to the Magic Castle for the first time and explaining to my parents that this isn't just a phase.

I will always be grateful for the Best, Lopez, and Hughes families. I so appreciate the love and care you have shown me—your homes have truly become second homes for me.

Thank you to my mentors: David Doyle, Steve Barnes, Scott Tokar, Dana Daniels, Taylor Hughes, Bob Dorian, Paul Dwork, and Diana Zimmerman. Thank you gents for teaching me how to be a better magician and speaker. I want to extend my gratitude to my two "magic mommas," Kate Ward and the late Joann Lawton. Thank you both for your support and encouragement at the Magic Castle.

I want to thank Kristi Hein (Pictures & Words) for being a fantastic editor.

Special thanks to Lisa Barbee (DesignsDoneNow.com) for your amazing design work.

A huge thanks to Mr. Crizz for all your laughter and help.

Lastly, I want to thank all of my friends throughout the years. Without all of you I would not be where I am today. And a huge thanks to all of my clients—actually, I think of you not as clients, but as family.

Inspiring Magic at Your Next Event!

Schedule Aaron O'Brien and make your next meeting a hit with everyone in your organization!

Tired of boring presentations at your virtual or live events? It's not easy to delight *everybody*.

But now you can. When you invite Aaron to entertain and motivate your audience, three things happen:

1. Your people will *thank you* for blowing their minds.
2. Your event will become magical *and* memorable.
3. You will enjoy working with Aaron as he personalizes his magic and message for your meeting.

> "We have hired Aaron more than 25 times for our company meetings. He never fails to *wow our team* and impress our customers. What I love the most is how he always customizes his presentation for event attendees. They LOVE it. And his magic is awesome too!! Highly Recommended. A++."
> —**KAREN MILLARD**, *Loyalty Program Advisor, Insperity*

Keynote Presentations • Zoom Meetings • Virtual Events
After-dinner Gatherings • Workshops & Seminars

Get Aaron on your Virtual or Live Event calendar right away. Call his booking coordinator, Brian McElreath: 707-774-5184. Or send an email: Hello@AaronObrien.com

www.ingramcontent.com/pod-product-compliance
Lightning Source LLC
LaVergne TN
LVHW041549070426
835507LV00011B/1006